These Devils Wore Blue

Blue

A Basketball Memoir

For Michael Kamal
Thanks for being a
good mentor for our
Friend Brad.
Go Duke

John Davis Cantwell, M.D.

John Cantwell MD
 # 24

authorHOUSE™

1663 LIBERTY DRIVE, SUITE 200
BLOOMINGTON, INDIANA 47403
(800) 839-8640
WWW.AUTHORHOUSE.COM

AuthorHouse™
1663 Liberty Drive
Bloomington, IN 47403
www.authorhouse.com
Phone: 1-800-839-8640

First published by AuthorHouse 3/15/2010

ISBN: 978-1-4208-6110-5 (sc)

Printed in the United States of America
Bloomington, Indiana

This book is printed on acid-free paper.

A NOTE ON THE TYPE

The type (or font) is Adobe Caslon, which Carol Twombly designed in 1990, based on the original creation by London type-maker William Caslon (1720s).

Benjamin Franklin selected it for the original printing of the Declaration of Independence.

Figure 1 - With my family

To:

Carson
Cameron
Blair
Hannah
Ashley
Mary Ellen

For all the joy you bring into my life, and Grandma's too.
I love you a lot, and wish you all the best in your own sporting experiences.

In memory of
Arthur Allen Cantwell, Jr., M.D.,
who taught me how to be a competitor,
and to
Jack Mullen
and
Doug Kistler
whose seasons ended prematurely, and who are remembered
fondly.

"...It is nothing at all like standing on the floor...as champions, with your fists raised, with the chills coursing up and down your spine, with your face aching from smiling, secure in the knowledge that all the work for all the years was worth it, and that on this night and for this season you are the best...

That is a thrill! It comes to a player only rarely and it comes only to those whose efforts and luck converge.

...these moments seem as if they happened only yesterday."
Bill Bradley
"Life on the Run"

TABLE OF CONTENTS

FOREWORD

Dr. Cantwell's 1960 Duke team sums up how the ACC tournament is a whole new season. Their championship has inspired many future ACC teams going into the tournament without having had a great regular season.

Knowing John personally as a friend and patient I can assure you this book will bring out the best in basketball and in life.

Bobby Cremins
Gatech Coach
1981-2000

PREFACE

Basketball was invented by a fellow physician, and at a YMCA like the one where I spent so much time as a youth learning some nuances of the sport.

The inventor, James Naismith, was Canadian by birth, of Scottish ancestry. Orphaned because of typhoid fever at age nine, he dropped out of high school at 15 to work on the family farm and in logging camps. He returned to school when he was 20, and eventually earned degrees in religion, physical education, and medicine.

In December 1891, while teaching at the International YMCA Training School in Springfield, Massachusetts, Naismith was asked by his director to devise an indoor game for the school's 40 students, to help keep them physically active between football season and the springtime activities of baseball and track.

Figure 2 - James Naismith, M.D.

The 30 year old Naismith recalled a game he used to play as a child, called "Duck on a Rock." It involved lobbing small stones up at a softball-sized rock on a boulder about 20 feet away. He got the idea of putting boxes (the janitor could only find peach baskets) on the ends of the indoor gymnasium, nailed 10 feet high on the overhead running track. A soccer ball was used initially. After a goal, the ball was either poked out of the basket with a pole or lifted out by someone on a step ladder.

Naismith scribbled a list of 13 rules in just an hour. The size of each team would depend on the square footage of the indoor (or outdoor) court, and could range from 5 to 9 individuals.

Only 1 basket was made in the 1st game, a 25-footer by William Chase, which would have been a 3-pointer today (and was then, as were free throws).

Graduates of the YMCA Training School took the new sport around the world in the next 30 years to over 70 international YMCAs. The game was fine-tuned as well over the ensuing years. Significant advances are noted in Table 1.

The 1st women's game was played in Springfield, Massachusetts, in 1894. Naismith's future wife, Maude Sherman, took part. For years, women's rules were different from men's, citing women's limited stamina and tendency to "hypertrophy of the heart." They were finally allowed to dribble in the 1950s, but only once. Their game became similar to the men's in the 1970s, culminating in their 1st Olympic exposure in 1976.

Naismith had received a BA degree from McGill in 1887, and added a divinity degree from nearby Presbyterian College. In 1895, he moved to Denver, to become head of physical education at the YMCA and to attend Gross Medical School (later to merge with the University of Colorado). He then took a job at the University of Kansas in 1898, where he lived with his wife and 2 of his total of 5 children. His job duties were unique, and well suited to him: direct the Chapel services, serve as athletic director and lead the new department of physical education. He soon became basketball and track coach. It is surprising he was not also asked to direct the student health center. His salary was $1,300.00 per year.

He never practiced medicine per se, but taught preventive medicine to students, especially adolescent development and sex education. He liked to gather data, taking 19 physical measurements (waist, shoulder size, arm span, and so forth) on every male freshman student.

In 1915, Naismith volunteered to join the Kansas National Guard, as a chaplain. He subsequently sailed to France with the

American Forces in September, 1917, at age 55, to give sex education lectures to the troops and to promote basketball tournaments, and spent a total of 19 months there.

In 1925, he and his wife became naturalized American citizens.

A hard worker, Naismith averaged only 4 hours of sleep per night. He never reaped financial reward from his basketball invention, and was not money-oriented to begin with, such that 2 of his home mortgages were foreclosed. A bit absent-minded, as some creative geniuses tend to be, he was known to forget that he had driven to work in his Model T and subsequently took the streetcar home.

As he neared the end of his life, James Naismith was recognized for what he had accomplished. His basketball rules were translated into 50 different languages and dialects. In 1936, basketball became an official part of the Olympic games, in Berlin.

Naismith could not have afforded a trip to Berlin on his meager salary. His friends organized "Naismith Nights," special basketball exhibition games which spread nationwide. A penny from each ticket sold was donated to "the doc's Olympic fund." He tossed up the center jump for the 1st game, and saw the United States team win gold medals by defeating Canada, outdoors in a rainstorm, 19 to 8.

Naismith's wife of 43 years died of a myocardial infarction the next year, and 2 months later he semi-retired from the University of Kansas at age 75. Oddly, he is the school's only basketball coach with a losing record (53 wins and 55 losses).

He remarried 2 years later, to a 56 year old Kansas fraternity house mother, but that union lasted only 4 months, for on November 19, 1939, Naismith had a stroke, seemed to recover, and then had a 2nd one that caused his death at age 78.

The sport he invented remains immensely popular, not just in the United States but throughout the world. In China alone, National Basketball Association game telecasts draw millions of viewers, and basketball courts dot the landscape of this country of 1.3 billion people.

A reporter recently traveled to one of the most remote areas in the world he could think of - Outer Mongolia. He approached an isolated yurt, in the middle of nowhere, and asked the occupant (via an interpreter) if he had ever heard of Michael Jordan. The man smiled and made a dribbling motion with his hands. Did he know who Michael played for, the reporter asked? Of course came the reply, the Chicago Yaks.

The following memoir is about my own experience with the game, beginning on my outdoor court, at the YMCA in the little Wisconsin town I grew up in, and during one notable season at Duke University.

TABLE 1
BASKETBALL MILESTONES

December 1891 - Game Invented.
1893 - 1st special ball manufactured.
1894 - 1st women's game.
1894-95 - Free throw introduced. Lane moved in from 20 ft. to 15 ft.
1895-96 - 2 points for a field goal, 1 for a free throw.
1896 - 1st college game with 5 on a side (Chicago vs. Iowa). 1st professional game.
1898 - Dribble legalized.
1908 - Limit of 5 fouls per player. Double dribble banned.
1921 - "Basket ball" changed to "basketball."
1923 - No designated free throw shooter allowed.
1932 - 3-second rule in free throw lane. 10-second limit to cross midcourt.
1933 - Started to eliminate the center jump after each score.
1936 - Hank Luisetti of Stanford brings the 1-handed shot to New York. 1st Olympic game.
1939 - 1st NCAA tournament (8 teams).
1943 - Kenny Sailors of Wyoming brings 1-handed jump shot to New York.
1967 - Dunking banned.
1972 - Freshmen allowed to play on the varsity.
1976 - Dunking reinstated. 1st women's game in Olympics.
1978 - Title IX elevation of college sports for women.
1985 - Shot clock installed.
1986-87 - 3-point shot line.

ACKNOWLEDGMENTS

I appreciate the cooperation of my former 1960 Duke teammates and coaches.

Anne Morgan did her usual excellent job in preparing the manuscript, despite my innumerable revisions.

Mike Moseley was very helpful in getting the figures on a disk.

I thank Jon Jackson and the Duke Sports Information Department, Bill Stagg of the Durham Herald-Sun, and the NC State Sports Information Department for permission to reproduce photographs.

The section on James Naismith was reproduced with permission of Elsevier and the American Journal of Cardiology (2004; 93: 1075-1077).

Coach Vic Bubas was kind enough to provide the afterword, and Bobby Cremins the foreword.

INTRODUCTION

In 1960, my Duke University basketball team finished the regular Atlantic Coast Conference (ACC) schedule with a mediocre 7-7 record. Included were three blowouts to arch-rival North Carolina, by margins of 26, 25 and 22 points, and sound defeats to Wake Forest by 19 and 17 points. Back then, the post-season ACC tournament meant everything. Win, and you progressed to the NCAA tournament. Lose, and your season ended. Even the National Invitational Tournament (NIT) in New York wasn't an option.

Our Duke team reported for the first pre-tournament practice still licking our wounds from the most recent defeat at home to U.N.C. The lights in the locker room were off. We dressed in the dark. And then our first-year coach, Vic Bubas, entered, turned on a small light and told us to sit down. He read a commitment contract he had drawn up, to the surprise of even the assistant coach, Fred Shabel. The contract stipulated that we would be focused and positive in our approach to the upcoming tournament, and agree to fully support each other. We would dive for all loose balls, and get every rebound possible. We wouldn't eat junk food. We would adhere to a curfew.

There were other items that I no longer recall. I do remember that each of us was to either sign the commitment or turn in our uniform and leave the room.

We all signed, and then prepared for intense practices. The starting lineup was reshuffled. I lost the starting guard position I had earned five games previously. In the process, however, I became a champion, Duke's first in the ACC, which is what a team sport is all about.

CHAPTER ONE
BEGINNINGS

The city of Shawano is nestled along the Wolf River in Mideastern Wisconsin, about 34 miles directly west of Green Bay. The Menominee Indians lived in the region before moving to a reservation nine miles away, in 1854. The name, Shawano, was coined in 1864, derived from a Menominee and Chippewa Indian word which translates "lake to the south." The Indians had a little village along the inlet, where the Wolf River runs into Shawano Lake. Not far from that site is the Shawano Community Hospital, where I was born and where my father worked as an obstetrician and generalist for 36 years. My brother, Art, a retired surgeon, lived just across the river from the inlet.

White men were first attracted to the area because of the logging potential. The first non-Indian to visit the Shawano region "paddled up the Wolf River in 1843 with a few men to scout out the area." He returned, to establish a sawmill.

My grandfather, William Hamilton Cantwell, came to Shawano from Milwaukee in 1869, two years before it officially became a village. He was 11 years old then, accompanied by his mother and older sister. He probably attended Lincoln School, a two-room structure built in 1872. I later attended an expanded version of that school.

Grandfather subsequently began working as an assistant to the local pharmacist and brother of the area's first permanent physician.

John Davis Cantwell, M.D.

He eventually opened his own pharmacy, added the job of postmaster, saved his money and attended Rush Medical School in Chicago, graduating in 1887.

He returned to Shawano the following year to begin a 50-year medical practice. He was vitally interested in sports, and served as manager (and team doctor, I'm sure) of the Shawano baseball squad. The team presented him with a gold-headed cane in 1888. My grandmother later gave the cane to me, long after Grandfather died.

In 1938, to commemorate his 50 years of service to the town, Grandfather was honored at the community hall where many of us honed our basketball skills as children. One of Grandfather's last public appearances, after he developed cardiovascular disease, was to attend the celebration of Shawano's Class-B State Championship basketball team in 1938.

Shawano repeated as all-class State Champions in 1940, led by Bill Reed, probably the city's greatest all-around athlete. Reed won 15 varsity letters in his high school career, not including baseball (the school did not have a team). He reached the major leagues in this sport, opening the 1952 season at second base for the Boston Braves.

I changed athletic gear as a tree changes the color of its leaves. In spring and summer, I oiled my baseball glove, donned a Philadelphia Phillies cap, and pounded doubles off the chicken-wire fence at the end of our vacant lot, just like big Del Ennis, the slugging outfielder of the "Whiz Kids."

In the fall, I would slip into a tattered football jersey, with the number 37 stenciled on it (the number worn by Doak Walker, the triple-threat halfback at Southern Methodist), and practice angling punts into the coffin corner and kicking field goals over the clothesline. The winter months were the longest, and probably explain why basketball was my favorite sport.

Figure 3 - Even at a young age I always had a ball of some type in my hands.

Ever since I can remember I've had a ball of some type in my hands. When I got a little older my main recollections include the snow, the ice in the nets and the cold wind blowing in from the west, across Wolf River.

Our home was on a high bank, where Indians obviously liked to camp in centuries past, given the arrowheads we would sometimes uncover while playing in the backyard.

To succeed in basketball in Wisconsin, as in other northern cities, you first had to learn to deal with the elements. The snow had to be shoveled off the driveway before Dad's and Mom's cars packed it down into ice, in which case it would then have to be laboriously chipped off. One cannot dribble well on an uneven surface, and slashing drives to the basket were part of my workout.

The net had to be whacked a few times with a broom to get the ice out and to loosen the cords. You also had to get up on step ladder and, using your elbows, stretch the net several times to keep the ball from sticking in it.

Clothing was dictated by the temperature. It could sometimes be as cold as -36 degrees Farenheit, but usually the temperature hovered around 0 degrees Farenheit or slightly above. I wore mittens, my wool stocking hat and a heavy coat, slightly large so it wouldn't constrict arm motion. The mittens would get wet and sloppy and take on a bit of an odor, all to my advantage when face guarding my two older brothers.

We wore rubbers, or galoshes, on our shoes in the late 1940s and early 1950s, to keep them from deteriorating.

When the weather was nice I would put on tennis shoes, as they were called in those days. Initially Mother tried to get me to wear a pair of my older sister's, stuffed with cotton in the toes to make them fit. I complained to my physician-father, and he took me to the K and G Sporting Goods Store on our tiny Main Street to buy some Keds. I really wanted to wear the white Converse Chuck Taylor Model, like the high school team wore, but they were more expensive.

I had several routines I followed each practice day. After free throws and driving lay ups, I would play a game of "golf," going around in a semi-circle to nine different spots. If I missed on the way to nine, I would have to start all over.

Set shots had evolved from the two-handed style to a push shot, raising the right leg. I got pretty good at that, and later found it a bit difficult to change to the planted right foot style. Free throws were shot underhanded. After several years, I also switched to the push shot, bouncing slightly on my toes.

The jump shot was in evolution. My older brothers, four and five years my senior, didn't shoot it very much in their days, but I saw it being used a lot when I started watching professional games on our new black and white television set.

After every high school game I saw I would come home, turn on the spotlight, and practice various shots or moves that I had seen until my mother would tell me it was time to go to bed. I would listen on the radio to the University of Wisconsin games and, during half time, head outside into the Wisconsin winter to emulate the play of Badger stars such as Dick Cable.

I looked forward to reading Sport magazine each month, especially the pre-season basketball all-American predictions, and plastered the walls in my tiny bedroom with pictures from the magazine. On my outdoor court I would pretend to be Tom Gola, LaSalle's great star, or Dick Ricketts or Sihugo Green, from Gola's rival, Duquesne University. I also liked Johnny O'Brien, Seattle's high scoring twin, especially because he was a little guy, about 5'9" in height. The initial pro players I tried to copy were Dolph Schayes of the Syracuse Nationals, the Boston Celtics Bob Cousy, and Slater Martin of the Minneapolis Lakers. Years later, during summer school at the University of Wisconsin, I would get to guard Cousy in a scrimmage.

Figure 4 - The scrimmage against Bob Cousy. I am shown under his arms. At the far right is D. Wayne Lucas, then an aspiring basketball coach, now a renowned horse trainer.

Cousy wanted to put on a fancy dribbling exhibition, and I was chosen to cover him. Rather than acting like the stooge I was supposed to be I pressured Cousy, tried for the steal, and clipped his arm. The ball bounced off his foot and rolled away. He wasn't happy about it.

As I entered my teenage years I read about incredible high scorers, like Bevo Francis of tiny Rio Grande College (who once scored 116 points in a game), and "Fabulous Frank" Selvy of Furman, who, from the guard position, swished a half-court shot against Newberry College for his 100th point of the night. For the season, he averaged about 40 points per game.

My older brothers would usually have a game going with their friends several times each week, and always included me. I learned how to play against older, taller opponents from these encounters.

Most small towns like ours had YMCAs. Ours was directed by Guy Booth and Arnie Gruber, who taught us the game of basketball, encouraged us in the Saturday morning games we played and admonished us for any unsportsmanlike actions.

We would often play "shirts and skins," with long underwear tops flopping on our behinds as we ran down the court.

Some of our high school stars, like Doug Page, would be working out as well on Saturdays after their Friday night encounters. As Page recalled recently, he'd have games of "21" against me, then a fourth or fifth grader, where you get two points for what would now be a three-pointer above the key, and one for the followup short shot. Play would often stop in the YMCA to watch our head-to-head battles.

I learned a lot from Page and other high school stars in Shawano, competing against him and watching his heads-up play in games. I wasn't surprised to hear much later that he had become a very successful high school basketball coach in the Green Bay area.

As we got into the seventh and eighth grades we had games and tournaments involving my Lincoln Public School team and the Catholic School (Sacred Heart), the Lutheran School (St. James), and the Indian School (Neopit). The games were usually close. Spectators sat along the sides of the court in folding chairs. The ceiling in the St. James gym was very low, such that you couldn't put too much arch on free throws. In the Lincoln School gym, the brick wall was at both end lines, curtailing aggressive lay ups.

There were rumors that the Indian kids would throw rocks at your bus if you beat their team, but I never saw this myself.

Three of the players from those four grade schools went on to play Division I college basketball. A fourth, 6'6" Fred Opperman, could have done likewise, but elected to take over his father's farm instead. Several others played for smaller colleges.

From these games we learned to play against top competition and under pressure-packed situations, a prerequisite for competing at the college level in the tough ACC.

Figure 5 - My 8th grade team. (I'm to the right of the ball.)

CHAPTER TWO
STATE CHAMPS

The high school basketball teams from my hometown of 5,000 were generally very good. However, they couldn't seem to get through the sectional tournament to reach the Elite 8 in the state tournament, held at the University of Wisconsin's Field House in Madison. It was the dream of probably every high school player in the state to win the state championship. There weren't any classes back in the 1950s, so smaller schools like ours would eventually face teams from Milwaukee, Madison or the Green Bay area as one progressed through the post-regular season games.

In 1956, the Shawano Indians High School basketball team ended the regular season with a second consecutive loss to the worst team in our own conference. Prospects for the upcoming tournament didn't seem overly bright, despite a respectable record of 14 wins and six losses.

However, over the next 2 1/3 seasons the team went on to win 60 of 64 games, including two all-class state championships and a third place finish. Two of the losses, to Two Rivers, were avenged in the state semifinals. The other two defeats were in slow-down games, one a triple overtime affair with Menasha, the other an overtime loss to Milwaukee North.

Hometown fans only saw one loss (to Two Rivers) during that remarkable run.

The main ingredients for the team's success were 1. Physical talent and 2. An excellent coach.

The talent included size, speed, inside and outside shooting ability, rebounding and free throw accuracy.

The captain of the 1956 team was guard Larry Maltbey, a 5'11" three-sport athlete, an unselfish type who could score when needed and who played an aggressive defense. I was the other guard, at just under 5'9", mainly an outside shooter.

The forwards were senior Guy Grignon, a Menominee Indian who, at 5'10", was undersized for his position. He made up for it with quickness, timing and a deadly shooting eye. Grignon was also a multi-sport athlete: track sprinter, football quarterback and switch-hitting outfielder.

Loren Wolf, at 6'4", was the classic forward, another unselfish performer who used his rebounding and passing skills to great advantage.

The center was the 6'6" Opperman, a 240 pound load in the middle, possessing a soft, accurate free throw touch and a little hook shot.

The top reserves in 1956 were 6'3" Dave Meyer, a football end, and leaping Mike Dodge, another 6'3" football receiver, a lefty who came off the bench both state championship years to provide a spark when the regulars tired or got into foul trouble. Marty Gharrity, a sophomore 6'2" guard, started slowly his first season but came on strong during the state tournament, hitting eight of nine crucial free throws in the championship game. The next year he blossomed into a scoring machine, and in his senior year set a single season scoring record that has lasted over 46 years and a state tournament single game record of 44 points that took 44 years for someone to break.

The coach was John Kenney, the son of Irish immigrants. I had known Coach Kenney since early childhood, as he had helped coach my older brothers. Once, as a little kid, I was playing hopscotch with my older sister and her friends. Coach Kenney happened to walk by. He paused, took in the scene and said: "I never thought I would see John Cantwell playing hopscotch." I was horrified. I have never played again, and never will, even with my grandchildren.

He used to teach physical education in the high school, and would sometimes come to Lincoln School to conduct a class. I was in the seventh grade. He had us do a speed and agility drill. He would try to catch you, encircle you in his arms, and then you would be eliminated. I was the last one he caught. I flipped up and out of his grasp, and sped away. He said that wasn't allowed, and didn't bother to chase after me. He made the rules, you see, I didn't.

Coach Kenney had been an assistant under Russ Owen, a terrific coach himself. Owen, a graduate of the Naval Academy, always had his teams wear coats and ties to away games, adding a touch of class with an attitude that if you look like a champion you might play like a champion. Kenney carried on this tradition when he became head coach in 1955-56.

He was very strict, but never overbearing, and had a dry sense of humor. He didn't tolerate unnecessary fancy passes. I can't recall him sniping at the referees.

He emphasized outside shooting drills and free throws. He used to put a dollar near the free throw line, a lot of money then, and the best shooter that day would pick it up. Years later, when I was coaching nine- and 10-year-old boys on a church-affiliated basketball team, I did the same drill.

Figure 6 - Members of our defending state championship team (left to right: Gharrity, Dodge, Opperman, Meyer, Wolf, Cantwell).

The 1957 team (figure 6) was probably the best in the school's history. Gharrity replaced Maltbey at guard, and Meyer took over for Grignon. Mike Dodge was the top reserve again, and started a crucial state tournament game when Opperman was out with the measles. Jerry Klose and Bernie Prusik added front court reserve height, while Tom Spohn and Harley Lyons filled in at guard. The team averaged 76 points per game to the opponent's 57. Five times the unit scored over 90 points and once over 100, despite resting the regulars when we were way ahead.

Figure 7 - The gold belt buckles that were given.

Each player in 1956 and again in 1957 was rewarded with a gold belt buckle (figure 7), commemorating the state titles. Letter jackets also reflected the championship efforts (figure 8).

Figure 8 – High school letter jacket.

The media coverage and fan support (figure 9) was tremendous. Home games were sell-outs, with vociferous audiences of 2,300.

Figure 9 – Newspaper headlines of our championship.

13

Highlights from the 1956 season included a school record 94 points in the season opener, an omen of things to come. A one-point victory over Marinette also stands out, as does the two-point win over West Allis Hale in the first state tournament contest. An earlier regional blowout of Clintonville, 86 to 50, avenged the two earlier regular season losses.

In 1957, the only two losses were to a tough, talented Two Rivers squad. Again, we got revenge in the tournament, knocking them out in the state semi-final encounter. Our team beat Wausau by only one point during the regular season. In the tournament, without Opperman because of the measles, we prevailed easily, 70-55.

Looking back at the championship seasons almost 50 years later several things seem apparent:

It takes a balanced team to win consistently. One superstar cannot do it alone.

A season has peaks and valleys. One cannot be discouraged by a loss even to an inferior team. You just have to learn from the encounter and prepare for the next opponent.

It is important to peak at the right time. Especially in 1956, Shawano kept gaining momentum as the tournament progressed. I would see this later during the 1960 Duke season.

It helps to have played in close games during the season. Good teams seem to find a way to win those. In one match-up against Wausau, the latter led virtually the whole game, except for the final seconds.

Good free throw shooters can make a difference. Our victory over Appleton in the 1956 state finals reflected that.

Key reserves are invaluable, when starters get fatigued, in foul trouble or ill with infectious diseases.

In 1958, we tried to "three-peat." Marty Gharrity and I were the only returning starters, but we added a 6'5" transfer center from Milwaukee, Norm Ostapinski, whose sister (whom he lived with) was hired as a teacher in Shawano. Gharrity had an incredible season, averaging 25.2 points per game and setting the state tournament single game record. I averaged nearly 19 points each game, while Ostapinski and forward Paul Timm were also in double figures.

Our team was rated #1 in the state the entire regular season. Our only loss was in the triple-overtime game with Menasha. In that game I tightened up on a one-and-one free throw with nine seconds to play and our team trailing by two points, but Paul Timm grabbed the rebound and put in a bank shot to tie the score. At the end of the first overtime I sunk a shot from mid court, which could have won the game, but the referee ruled that the ball had left my hand a fraction of a second before the horn sounded. The third overtime was a free throw contest. Our team made four of five, but our opponents made all five. Ironically, Timm was our only player to miss.

The very next night we had another game, this one at home against Wausau, then the second ranked team in the state. We won a close game, aided by Gharrity's 28 points, to maintain our top ranking.

Figure 10 - With Coach Rudy Ellis during state tournament competition my senior year.

In the state tournament (figure 10) we won the first game, a high-scoring affair with Eau Claire, 90 to 81, a game in which Gharrity set the record. The next night we faced a black team from Milwaukee North, who emphasized defense and low scoring games.

The score was tied with seconds to go. As the senior shooting guard, I wanted the ball in my hands and planned a final drive to the basket. I asked the other guard, sophomore Harley Lyons, to let me know when there were five seconds on the overhead clock (I couldn't look up for fear the ball would be stripped from me by their tenacious defenders). With the roar of the 13,000 fans, I couldn't hear Harley, and made my move too late to get a shot off or to draw a foul. In retrospect, I should have had him use hand signals.

In any event, we lost in overtime. We did bounce back the next day to stifle Madison West and their star guard, Jim Bakken (who still holds the pro football single game field goal record of seven), taking home the third place trophy.

After I scored 26 points against Madison West, and held Bakken to four, the Wisconsin coach Bud Foster seemed more interested in me.

CHAPTER THREE
A WALK-ON AT
DUKE UNIVERSITY

Although our high school team had done well, and I had set the career basketball scoring record and made the all-state tournament first team twice, I wasn't heavily recruited, most likely due to my lack of height. I had received a lot of correspondence from smaller college coaches throughout the Midwest, but wanted to test myself against Division I standards.

I did get a scholarship offer from Valparaiso to play football, and was finally offered a basketball scholarship by Wisconsin's coach Foster. Their team played an old-style controlled game, while I preferred a pressing, fast-breaking approach, so I didn't take the offer seriously.

I was always intrigued by the South as a youth, mainly the warmer weather, but also the stately mansions, tales of plantation life, and cotton fields. I didn't fully realize how abusive the area was to blacks, as I didn't grow up with them, and didn't even know any.

I had read about Dick Groat, Duke's all-American in the two sports, basketball and baseball, I wanted to pursue. (I later got to guard Groat in basketball scrimmages, when he would stop by Duke en route to spring training with the Pittsburgh Pirates). I also recall a feature article on the school in Time Magazine, depicting the beautiful gardens and attractive coeds.

As the youngest of four children, I wanted to break out of the mold, to do something different. My brothers had attended Wisconsin, and I had enjoyed visiting them, taking in the Kappa Sigma fraternity parties and the college football and basketball games. Classes were very large in this school of 30,000 to 40,000 students, and I wanted something smaller. Duke had an enrollment of around 5,000, the size of my hometown, limited class sizes to 24, and had a good pre-medical program.

The only downside I could see was that Duke was 1,000 miles from where I lived, and I didn't know a single person there. The only time I had ever been away from home alone in my 18 years was to attend a boys camp for a week, just nine miles away. I got terribly homesick.

Dad and I flew to Durham the spring of my senior year to visit Duke, and also Virginia (where Dad's former college roommate at Wisconsin was the athletic director). It was my first plane trip, a North Central propeller job in which you had to walk up hill to reach your seat.

The Duke campus was beautiful in the springtime. I met Fred Shabel, the affable assistant coach, who introduced me to several sophomore basketball players including Fred Kast, John Frye and Howard Hurt.

Coach Shabel explained that Duke only had four basketball scholarships to give each year, and had committed all for the coming season. It wasn't a big deal to us, as Dad actually preferred that I not be on scholarship so that I would have more leeway if my pre-medical studies and laboratories conflicted with basketball practice.

Years later I read where noted announcer Billy Packer blamed me from keeping him from going to Duke, which was his initial choice. Supposedly the Duke coaches told Packer that they were thinking of giving me a scholarship. I guess a fifth one was available and I suppose that they were just trying to get Packer to hasten his decision to attend Duke. Instead, it had the opposite effect. Packer got angry, signed with Wake Forest, and vowed to make life miserable for Duke and for me (which he usually did).

The trip to Virginia was interesting. The campus was as attractive as Duke's, and the school teemed with Mr. Jefferson's touch, and his legacy.

Unlike Duke, which takes students from all over the country, most of the Virginia students I met were from the South.

The team captain, a friendly guy, took me to a cabin party, along with his gorgeous date. The latter gave me a first-class kiss, smack on the lips, at the end of the evening.

At the cabin party I observed two of the Virginia basketball players engaged in a loud argument as to whose was longer. They loosened their pants and removed their belts. I didn't know what to expect. They then held their belts up for comparison, declared one the winner, and smiled at the crowd who had anticipated something more raucous.

I decided that parties might be more interesting at Virginia, but I preferred Duke with a better mix of students. I would later have to guard one of the Virginia "belt-length" participants, a high-scorer who provided a real challenge to me.

My parents drove me to college. Most of my clothes were packed in a large container and sent by truck. The container went to some other destination and, after many phone calls and letters, finally arrived several months later.

Freshman couldn't have cars at Duke then, so I had to sell my 1955 Ford two-door coupe, with its Hollywood muffler. In retrospect, I should have kept it, as it was a great car.

I checked into my dormitory room, only to find both closets filled with my roommate's clothes. He was blond, good-natured, and apparently wealthy, fresh from prep school. Thinking that he might want to try out for the Duke football team, he had brought along his own shoulder pads from prep school, which did not seem like a good idea to me. We went down to watch practice one day, a nut-cracker-type drill of one-on-one pounding, and he subsequently thought better of his original idea.

My parents lingered a few days, enjoying the Duke campus and taking me out for dinner in Durham or in Chapel Hill. One day I came back to my dorm room from a class, observing a note that had been tacked to the door:

"We have to get home.
Study hard and give it your all.
We love you. See you at Christmas."
Dad and Mom.

I gulped a time or two and settled in for a long separation from them. I think, in retrospect, that they left early to avoid any emotional outpouring on their end, and possibly on mine. They were now empty-nesters, a big transition to face.

Duke freshman had to wear little beanies the first few months of school and were not allowed to associate with fraternity guys or to ride in their cars. We also had Saturday classes.

My social life was dismal. I wasn't a ball of fire to begin with in this department, as I was rather shy. The girl-to-boy ratio of 3-4:1 didn't help matters either. The few cute girls were snapped up by the likes of the Betas, Phi Delts or KA's, who cruised about in Chevy Impala convertibles, Thunderbirds and the like.

I did meet one girl whom I was attracted to. She had dates lined up so far in advance that I hardly saw her more than on two or three occasions. I thought about asking her to attend the Duke chapel services with me on Sundays, but am glad that I didn't as I learned later that she was Jewish.

All freshman students had to take swimming, in physical education (PE) classes.

The instructor was the varsity swim coach, a rather loud sarcastic type. I'm not a good swimmer, which the coach didn't seem to appreciate. I couldn't float, given my body composition, further irritating him. The only thing I passed was the racing dive, why I'll never know.

It was of great satisfaction to me when one day I approached the instructor and handed him a note, stating that I was to be excused from swimming hereafter due to basketball and then baseball practice. He couldn't believe it, thinking (I'm sure) that I was a total klutz.

It also elevated my PE grade to an A, which was automatic if you were participating in a sport.

I meandered down to Cameron Indoor Stadium for some pick-up basketball games before the October 15th regular pre-season practices began. I met the four scholarship players. Fred Schmidt had been the most valuable high school player in Philadelphia, an award previously won by Wilt Chamberlain. Buzz Mewhort, from Toledo, had set the all-time scoring record at his high school and was the other forward. The center was Charlie Raksnis, who had a neat little scoop shot but who wouldn't have been a starter on my high school team. The guard was Jack Mullen, a 24 year old who had just gotten out of the Navy, after making the all-Navy basketball squad. Jack had long arms and was a tenacious defender, a true point guard before the term was popularized. Several others were aggressively vying for the fifth starter spot.

I arrived pretty much unannounced. After several weeks freshman coach, Whit Cobb, mentioned that he had received a letter from my high school coach my senior year, Rudy Ellis, after which I seemed to be given more careful scrutiny.

When regular practices began, Coach Cobb instilled a new drill. The player with the ball was to start above the key and drive right into the defender, who moved up from the baseline. It reminded me of football drills in high school and was obviously a test of our physical toughness.

I drove hard into the first defender, like the running back that I was, and sent him backwards. The next round Buzz Mewhort flung me aside like a suitcase. I moved ahead of the player in front of me during round three, to get another crack at Buzz, but Coach Cobb sensed what was going on and called the drill off. We never did it again.

Our first game as freshmen was against Billy Packer and Wake Forest, powered by 6'8" center Len Chappell. We won, and I managed to score 15 points. Packer grabbed me from behind, late in the game, to draw an intentional foul in hopes that I would miss a free throw. I couldn't see who was on my back, thinking it might be an irate fan, and tried to shake him off, throwing back a few elbows. It was our only moment of glory against Wake Forest that year, as we had to play them three more times and lost every one.

My best game was against VPI. Dad had flown down, unannounced, to surprise me, but I spotted him the instant he entered the crowded gym. I was able to score 23 points, putting on a show for him and leading our team to a win. My other good game was against North Carolina, led by guards Donnie Walsh and Yogi Poteet. I scored 22 that night and we won, our ninth victory of the season versus seven defeats.

With our tallest player, Mewhort, only 6'4", we were usually out-manned under the boards, despite his aggressive play.

For the season, Schmidt was the top scorer, averaging 17 points. Mewhort followed with 13.4 points per game, and I was third with 10. (figures 11, 12)

Figure 11 – The Duke freshman team. I'm number 12, Jack Mullen is 23. My roommate Jerry Butler is 11. Fred Schmidt is 2nd from the right in the last row.

FIgure 12 - Dunking freshman year (helped by a springboard).

Whit Cobb was an interesting coach. A suave single guy, he seemed to have girlfriends in every city we visited, usually borrowing a dime from one of us to make his phone calls to them.

In baseball I started at second base on the freshman team, but later requested to be shifted to the pitching staff, where I felt I had the best chance to succeed.

Unlike basketball, where you learned something every day in practice, I got very little help from the baseball coaching staff. The only positive advise I received was during the very first game, when I led off with a single and reached first base. The manager was coaching there and warned me about the left-handed pitcher's pick-off move. I nodded in agreement, and promptly was picked off on the very first attempt.

I made the varsity baseball team as a sophomore, but didn't see any action. I was far behind in my pre-medical laboratory work, because of the post-season basketball tournament, and had to miss several road trips in which I might have had an opportunity to pitch.

The baseball team traveled by bus and meals were in cafeterias, a far cry from the first-class arrangements we had received in basketball.

I made the trip with the team on spring break, riding over night in our crowded bus to Winter Haven, Florida, where we practiced next to the Washington Senators and played games against Rollins College.

One night, before our game the next day, we tried to sneak some Rollins girls out of their sorority windows to party with us along the lake front. Unfortunately, my date was a bit heavy, and couldn't be pulled through the window, so I went back to our dorm to practice my pitching motion. One of my teammates, from California, had better success, and stayed out most of the night with his date. The next night he was roused from his stupor on the bench to pinch hit. Still in a fog, he stood at the plate, watched three straight strikes zip by, and dragged back to the dugout.

I dropped baseball my junior year, as it took up too much of my time and was interfering with the grades I needed to get into medical school. I then started studying some afternoons in the Duke Gardens, reading my English major assignments which included the poems of Emily Dickinson and the prose of Thomas Hardy. I found that I didn't miss baseball as much as I thought I would.

I spent the summer months after freshman year working as a Coca-Cola route salesman. I wore a golden-brown uniform with my name on it. Kids along the route would wave and invariably holler "hey, Coke man."

I started work early and usually finished by mid-afternoon. I was given a key to the high school gym, so I could work on my game every day. I mainly wanted to develop longer range on my jump shots, and to improve my left-handed dribbling. I'd also add situps and pushups when I got home, and then run "the bridges," a two-mile circuit which crossed the Wolf River twice.

I needed to be in top shape to make the varsity, as there were a lot of returning lettermen.

Duke changed basketball coaches between my freshman and sophomore years. Harold Bradley left to become head coach at Texas. North Carolina State assistant coach, Vic Bubas, was hired to replace him.

One of the first things Coach Bubas did was to meet individually with each returning player. He promised that all varsity positions were wide-open, irrespective of scholarship status.

Tryouts were held in October, 1959. We scrimmaged, under the watchful eyes of Bubas, Fred Shabel and new freshman coach and varsity assistant, Bucky Waters.

My roommate, a second-string guard on the freshman team, saw that he had virtually no chance to make the varsity and offered to slack off when guarding me so that I could get more shots and show what I could do. I declined his kind sacrifice, told him to play his usual way, and made the squad anyway as Bubas, true to his word, cut the returning co-captain. I called my parents (the operator thought I was kidding when I told her the home phone number was "4") and they were equally thrilled.

CHAPTER FOUR
THE 1960 DUKE TEAM

The 1960 Duke basketball team members represented eight different states, mainly along the east coast. Nine had earned all-state honors in high school. Four had been on state championship teams. Buzz Mewhort and I were the only Midwesterners.

Howard Hurt, (figure 13) the 6'2½" captain of the team, played at Woodrow Wilson High School in Beckley, West Virginia, and also had a year of prep school at the Greenbriar Military School in Lewisburg, West Virginia.

Figure 13 - Howard Hurt.

His high school basketball team won the West Virginia state championship in 1954, and his prep school had similar honors in 1957.

He won all-state honors in both football and basketball, and once in track.

Although he was under-sized for a forward, he more than compensated with his aggressiveness and toughness.

We were members of the same Phi Delta Theta fraternity. A group of pledges, usually a dozen or so, would gang up on an active member late at night, subdue him, and carry him off to be dunked in a shallow pool on the Duke campus. I thought I had put up a good fight before I was overcome. Howard broke the first pledge's arm! They promptly reassessed the situation and decided not to bother him again.

Figure 14 – Doug Albright.

Doug Albright, (figure 14) attended Greensboro Senior High School in North Carolina, where he was the leading scorer and rebounder in 1957 and a member of the Greensboro Daily News All-State Basketball Team.

A solid 6'5", 200 pounder, he battled under the basket every practice, pushing the first-stringers.

Nicknamed "Chowman," he helped pay his way through college by working in the evenings selling sandwiches, snacks and soft drinks around the west campus quadrangles, hollering, "Chowman" to alert us to his presence.

Larry Bateman (figure 15) was also an all-state basketball player at Greensboro High School and participated as an all-star in the annual East-West game.

Figure 15 - Larry Bateman.

His time at Duke was interrupted by four years in the Air Force. When he first attended Duke, assistant coach Fred Shabel was a member of the team.

A 6'6", 215-pound bruiser, Larry (like Doug Albright) enjoyed hard-nosed practice sessions, making the starters even better in the process. He also added a delightful sense of humor.

Fred Kast (figure 16), part of the stellar freshman recruiting class of 1961, earned all-state honors two years at Rahway High School in New Jersey. In 1957 his team won the state championship and he received honorable mention all-American honors. He still holds the school's career basketball scoring record of 1,312 points and the single game record of 41 points.

Figure 16 – Fred Kast.

In baseball, Fred was a pitcher on a team that won the county and state tournament titles in 1957. He made the all-county team and was an honorable mention all-state selection.

Charles B. "C.B." Johnson (figure 17) was a four-sport star at Isadore Newman High School in New Orleans. In addition to basketball and football, he also competed in track and golf. His basketball team won the state championship in 1955. C.B. earned all-state basketball honors for three years.

Figure 17 - C.B. Johnson.

At a shade under 6'3", he was undersized for a college forward, and not quick enough for the guard position. His football toughness was apparent as he held his own against taller colleagues in our daily practice sessions.

Donald "Buzz" Mewhort (figure 18) was heavily recruited out of DeVilbiss High School in Toledo, Ohio, where he was an all-city basketball player his junior and senior years and a second-team all-state selection senior year (Jerry Lucas and John Havlicek were contemporaries). By the time he graduated he set the DeVilbiss High School career scoring record.

Figure 18 - Buzz Mewhort.

A 6'4", 200 pounder, Buzz added stability to a talented, younger team his senior year and served as co-captain with all-American Art Heyman.

Buzz and I roomed together on road trips. If we didn't get to play much in the games we'd come back to the hotel, still with a lot of adrenaline circulating, and sometimes wrestle to settle down. I got him hooked on malted milk tablets, until his weight started ballooning and he realized why.

Buzz would occasionally puff on a cigarette early on, in the bathroom. His dad, a former college athlete, referee and no-nonsense guy, happened to appear once, unannounced. He needed to use the restroom, smelled the cigarettes smoke, and later asked Buzz about it. Buzz's first inclination was to blame it on me, but his dad didn't buy that so he confessed.

Merrill Morgan (figure 19), a 6'2½" guard, was one of the last of the two-handed set shot cagers at Montclair High School in New Jersey, where his team won the conference championship and he was named the outstanding player in Essex County.

Figure 19 – Merrill Morgan.

Merrill's personal moment of college glory came in 1959. At the last minute, before the Duke team was to fly to Philadelphia for a double-header against Pennsylvania and Villanova, walk-on Morgan was added to the traveling squad.

During the Friday night game against Penn, there wasn't enough room on the bench, so Merrill had to sit in the next row.

On Saturday, Howard Hurt became ill. The Duke coaches decided to start Morgan in his place, against an excellent Villanova team in the Palestra, a team led by all-American George Raveling.

Shaking hands with the opponents before the game, Morgan recalls one of them asking him "Where were you last night?"

Villanova played a 2-1-2 zone defense. Merrill proceeded to make eight two-handed set shots (from today's 3-point range), which, combined with a lay up and two free throws, gave him a 20-point evening.

The very next game was in the Dixie Classic, against Michigan State and "Jumping" Johnny Green. Merrill again started the game. Within two seconds he had a jump ball with Green, "who outjumped me by three feet." He soon thereafter returned to the bench.

Carroll Youngkin (figure 20) was one of the stars on the team, a strapping 6'6" 200 pounder who reminded me of Gary Cooper in the movie "High Noon." He didn't waste words and delivered when the situation called for it. He was a two-time all-state performer at North Davidson High School in North Carolina and somehow got away from nearby Wake Forest and their colorful coach, "Bones" McKinney.

Figure 20 - Carroll Youngkin.

Once, on a bus ride to play North Carolina, Coach Bubas circulated an unsigned postcard from a disgruntled fan, telling how sorry we all were. When the card got to Youngkin, he glanced at it, rolled down his window, and threw it out. Later, Bubas was wondering what happened to his card. Nobody seemed to know.

Carroll once pulled an "all-nighter," cramming for an exam, probably aided by something like NoDoz. He wound up writing a long essay in his blue book on a new bowling alley on the outskirts of Durham, totally unrelated to the questions asked. I believe that he got an opportunity to retake the examination.

Doug Kistler (figure 21), at 6'8½" the tallest player on the team, competed at Radnor High School in Wayne, Pennsylvania, and also subsequently at Peddie Prep School in New Jersey. He earned all-state honors in both states.

Figure 21- Doug Kistler.

In addition to basketball, Doug played offensive and defensive end on the football team his senior year, and played the drums in high school and with a swing band.

Nicknamed "Biggie," he saved his best games for the ACC tournament in 1960, where he was named the most valuable player.

John Frye (figure 22) had a storybook career at Huntington East High School in West Virginia.

Figure 22 – John Frye.

As a junior, he made the all-state basketball team, along with Howard Hurt and Jerry West. In his senior year he was named captain of the all-state squad.

He was also named captain of the all-state football team and received the Kennedy Award as the most outstanding player in West Virginia.

In baseball, he is a member of the all-state second team. In track, he tied for fifth place in the state high-jump competition and was selected to the all-state track team.

In addition, he was elected President of Boy's Nation, a group of the best all-around students and athletes from the United States.

Frye's and Hurt's basketball teams competed against each other their junior year, in Huntington. One of the latter's coaches allegedly turned the heat up very high in the gym, hoping it would have adverse effects on Hurt's squad, to no avail.

In Frye's senior basketball season, his team faced Jerry West's East Bank High School unit in the regional finals. Ahead by one point, with four seconds to go, there was a jump ball at center court. As Frye recalls, "East Bank got the tip in the back court and drove all the way to make the winning basket. The timekeeper forgot to turn the clock on."

At Duke, John was married, with a little boy, Johnny Rex. A pre-Divinity student, we fought to sit next to him when our Piedmont Charter flight hit turbulent weather, thinking that maybe our chances of survival would be enhanced.

I was nicknamed "Dachshund" (figure 23) because of my short legs. During a freshman game at Virginia, Frye and Hurt discovered an old dachshund in the basement of the field house. Sneaking into my locker, they outfitted the dog in jersey #24 and set him loose on the main floor during intermission. The dog must have gotten a little excited, for my uniform had a somewhat pungent odor that kept my opponent at bay during the varsity game.

Figure 23 - John Cantwell.

Another of my nicknames was "Stump." Once, I was walking to class when "Moose" Bosson, a Kappa Sig football lineman, hollered across the quad, "hey kid, go back to your room. You forgot your legs."

The teasing was all in good fun, something I still observe in the Atlanta Braves' locker room many years later.

Charles Francis "Jack" Mullen, Jr. (figure 24) was the scholarship 5'11" guard on my freshman team. As mentioned earlier, he was older, having spent four years in the Navy.

Figure 24 - Jack Mullen.

Jack was born in Weissport, Pennsylvania, and attended Lehighton High School. In addition to basketball, he also started in baseball (and played two years of both sports at Duke). He was nicknamed "Tubes," because of all the time he spent watching TV.

During our freshman practices I had never seen a defender play with the intensity that Jack had. It made me better, just watching him and having to go against him in one-on-one drills.

Jay Beal (figure 25), at 5'11" was probably the best shooter on the team. He had been a basketball and baseball star at Wethersfield High

School in New Jersey and then had attended Cheshire Academy. He was named captain of both teams.

Figure 25 - Jay Beal.

He was later notorious for "horse" games with Coach Shabel. He loved the game and played the year around. He is still putting up his little squirt jump shots in Mobile, a lifelong "gym rat."

Beal had a slightly protruding front tooth and thus his nickname was "Beaver." Another nickname was "Pigfingers," for his small hands. His crew cut exposed a very round head, and we would try to palm it as one does a basketball, when he least expected it, sneaking up on him in the library or catching him out on a date. No wonder he doesn't attend our reunions or respond to any letters.

While I was heavily engaged in my pre-medical studies and athletic endeavors in 1960, four black freshman at North Carolina A&T State University were up to far more important things. Franklin McCain, Joseph McNeil, Ezell Blair, Jr., and David Richmond, were staging a sit-in at the "whites only" lunch counter at the downtown Woolworth store in Greensboro, N.C.

Their highly courageous action helped change the course of civil rights history.

In what spare time I had I read about their protest, and similar other attempts by blacks to salvage their rights and their dignity.

I could have boycotted the single downtown movie theater in Durham, as some were doing, sending the theater operators a message that blacks should be given equal access to the theater as whites were.

I didn't join the protest and, looking back, wish that I had.

My baseball activities were interrupted one long spring weekend when I went through "Hell Night" with the other pledges of the Phi Delta Theta fraternity. It was our final initiation, before we would become active members.

We were told to wear old clothes, and to report around 7 p.m. The active members put molasses and some kind of powder all over my clothes, and began force-feeding me chewing tobacco. I could not chew fast enough, and wound up swallowing a lot, which shortly thereafter induced severe nausea and vomiting.

We were then divided into groups of four, given our assignment for the next two days, and dropped off in some wooded area a ways from the campus.

We made our way back, borrowed a car, and set off to find the four items that were necessary for us to become fraternity members. The items included:

1. An autographed brassiere from a coed at Converse College in Spartanburg, S.C., who had just ended a stormy relationship with one of the senior Phi Delts, and never wanted to see him again.

2. A quart jar of fish maggots.

3. A three-hole outdoor john seat.

4. A 12-foot boat.

We rolled into Converse College the next day, found the girl, and after a lot of pleading, got her to autograph one of her bras for the "jerk" she had just broken up with.

Along the South Carolina coast we located a marine shop that specialized in fishing gear and bait. They did have fish maggots, I'm not sure why, which we crammed into a quart jar.

The three-hole outdoor john seat was harder to find. We visited every outhouse we came across, as we meandered through the Carolinas, and found that most were one- or two-hole jobs. Finally, during Sunday morning worship services at a black church (with gospel singing emanating from the open windows) we hit the jackpot, pulling and hammering on the triple seater until it broke free, and stuffed it in our trunk.

On the way back to Duke we scrutinized every yard we passed for a boat. We finally found one, late Sunday afternoon, which looked about 12 feet in length. Gary Wilson, a smooth-talking football player, took control. He knocked on the door and spoke with the house sitter, staying at the place while the owners were away. Gary explained that he was their nephew, and had come to pick up the boat. The nice occupant even helped us attach the boat trailer to our car.

Gary Wilson later became the Chief Financial Officer for the Marriott Corporation and then Walt Disney Enterprises. He now is the co-owner of Northwest Airlines.

I don't recall if we ever returned the boat. I hope that we did.

CHAPTER FIVE
THE DUKE BASKETBALL
COACHES

Vic Bubas (figures 26, 27) was red-haired, handsome, articulate and earnest. He had a measured speech without any "ands" or "ahs." He also had beautiful penmanship, and still does.

Figure 26 - Vic Bubas as an N.C. State player.

Figure 27 - Left to right: Coaches Shabel, Bubas, and Waters.

He had played under Coach Everett Case at N.C. State. During his four years there, from 1948-1951, the team won 111 games and lost only 24, winning the Southern Conference Championship each year and reaching the Final Four in 1951. Bubas twice earned all-conference honors, and, as a senior, was named to the Golden Chain for leadership and scholarship.

He had learned a lot from Coach Case. At times, while playing N.C. State, it felt like we were scrimmaging against ourselves, so similar were the offensive plays.

Bubas's practices were meticulously planned, which was fine with me. With my heavy pre-medical laboratory schedule, I could not afford to waste a minute. Vic had Cameron Indoor Stadium repainted and repaired. He organized a "ladies night," where he introduced each player, explained nuances of the game, had us demonstrate various shots and showcased us in a scrimmage. Afterwards, we visited with some of the 1,000 ladies in attendance and signed autographs.

Coach Bubas had a controlled intensity about him (figure 28). He didn't shout, rant or swear. He also didn't whine to the officials. When he spoke of the "burning to win" feeling we should all have in our abdomens I practically had to take Maalox to control mine.

Figure 28 – The Duke coaches in action. Buzz Mewhort is on the left.

He once gave a pre-game speech and demonstrated the difference between an individual effort versus a team approach, using a book of matches. He lit a single match, with the resulting small flame, and then ignited the rest of the matchbook. The flames shot up from his hand. I was afraid he might get a severe burn. We all got the message, however.

He never belittled players, nor was he physically or verbally abusive. The only time I saw him even touch a player in a forceful way was right before a big home game. Our forwards and center were seated. He went down the line, asking them if they could "take it" physically. They nodded that they could, without much enthusiasm. He proceeded to give each one a little smack on the cheek and then ask if they could take that. It got them riled up, ready to play.

In practice he had a pair of lace panties which one of the big men would wear if they weren't pounding the boards hard enough on rebounds. He didn't have to use it very often, as the effect was usually apparent.

On rare occasions, he would have us stand at one end of the court. He would throw a basketball high in the air, in the middle of us, and say that he wanted the toughest guy to bring the ball back to him. I didn't think that it was a very fair contest as one of the 6'6", 6'7" or 6'8½" players would pluck the ball out of the air, shield it with his body and run it back to him. If he had rolled it towards us I might have had a chance.

Captain Howard Hurt recalls Bubas as "a great organizer and motivator. He was young and we all wanted to be like him - dress like him, talk like him, etc. His leadership lessons and discipline and persistence have stayed with me well over the years."

To Buzz Mewhort, Vic was "the most mature 32 year old I have ever known. His motto of 'discipline, desire, sacrifice and organization' accurately described him and ultimately his teams. He was always under control and in charge on the bench, and usually in practice. Only rarely did the red-head's temper come out in practice and, even then, it was calculated to motivate those of us who needed motivation. He was a true leader for whom you always wanted to play your best and for whom an 'atta boy' was treasured."

Fred Kast credits Bubas with "the beginning of Duke basketball's success as we know it today." His easy-going manner belied an underlying intensity. Fred still smiles at Vic's "pump and take your beating" big man approach to the game.

Merrill Morgan, Howard Hurt, and Doug Kistler all became basketball coaches. Merrill recently spoke with legendary high school coach, Morgan Wootten, at one of the latter's clinics. To Wootten, Vic Bubas "was a coach ahead of his time," especially with his superbly organized recruiting methods, beginning with high school undergraduates.

Doug Albright states that Bubas's coaching lessons "turned out in many cases to be life lessons." He was not just a great coach - he was a great person who "could have been successful in just about any area he chose, be it business, sports administration, or other professional pursuits. He was a powerful mentor in how we should compete, and how we should live."

Psychologist John Frye recalls new coach Vic Bubas as being "young, energetic, and charismatic." He was a "high task" person, while assistant coach Shabel was a "high relationship" type.

John's thesis on leadership reported that "close to 90% of the productivity of any group is attributed to the two principles of task orientation and relationship orientation."

He is quick to add that Bubas was also very personable, but was a leader whose task (or goal) came first and the relationship second.

Shabel was also task oriented, "but he added the relationship quality each day. He would kid with us, play horse and tennis with us, etc." Together they were a powerful team, complimented also by Bucky Waters, who was able to combine both task and relationship effectively.

Assistant coach Fred Shabel, as Frye notes, was someone you could discuss things with when you didn't want to go to the head guy. He was probably the best horse player I have ever seen.

Shabel grew up in New Jersey where his basketball team won the county championship and he made the all-county team. (A teammate was Togo Palazzi, who was an all-American at Holy Cross and then a Boston Celtic.) He came to Duke in 1950 and played on the freshman team. The next season he played behind all-American guard Dick Groat, but was a starter for the Blue Devils in the 1952-53 season. His senior year he and Joe Belmont shared the starting assignment.

He went into the Air Force after graduating from college and was subsequently named basketball coach at Shaw, South Carolina, Air Force Base. He also coached the Air Force All-Stars in Denver, Colorado.

He was project officer for the United States Olympic Basketball Team in 1956, working with the team's training program and schedule until the squad departed for Australia.

After his two years of duty in the military, he was hired by Esso Standard Oil and worked in sales for that company in Elizabeth, New Jersey, until hired by Duke to be an assistant.

Many of our players were partial to Fred because he had recruited them. To Buzz Mewhort, "Shabel's energy and savvy coaching on defense ('peck, peck, peck') was a nice complement to Bubas's more controlled style. Shabel was a winner who engendered a willingness among the players to follow his advise in all things."

At our post-season banquet in 1960, Coach Shabel said something that has always remained in my mind. He indicated that life in general was a lot like our basketball season, with some peaks and valleys. We should remember what brought us success, despite the down moments, things like hard work, staying focused, and remaining self-confident, and apply the same formula to life's many challenges. I would do just that when faced, years later, with the trials, tribulations and joys of having a severely retarded child.

The only thing that he said that I disagreed with at the time, and still do today, was during my junior year. I didn't like being relegated to the bench, and told him that I wanted to play more. His answer was that in five years it really wouldn't make that much difference. On the contrary, it is important, I still think, to live in the moment, to seize each opportunity and get the very most out of it, because you only pass through each phase of life once.

R.C. "Bucky" Waters was from Collingswood, New Jersey, where he was all-state in football, basketball, and baseball, and subsequently a member of the school's sports Hall of Fame. He had played basketball at N.C. State under Everett Case and Vic Bubas, and was hired by the latter to coach the freshman and to be an assistant varsity coach at Duke, at age 24. Previously he had coached Ashe Central High School in Jefferson, N.C., to the Parkway Conference championship, the first in the history of the school.

An effervescent man, Bucky was hard-working and patient, like Bubas and Shabel. I can still recall his admonition to play defense "like mean jungle cats."

Eddie Cameron, for whom the stadium was named, was the athletic director. He had been a star in football, basketball, and track at Culver Military Academy, and at Washington and Lee University.

He was head basketball coach at Duke from 1929 to 1943, guiding the Blue Devils to three Southern Conference championships.

When football coach, Wallace Wade, left for the Army in 1942, Cameron took over as acting coach and also began his long career as athletic director.

I only talked to him once, during my career at Duke, and it wasn't by my choice.

My junior year we were playing North Carolina at Duke. Both teams were rated in the top 10. We were powered by the sophomore New Yorker, Art Heyman. They had several New York players as well, part of coach Frank McGuire's "underground railroad" to U.N.C. The New York players had been rivals in high school. No love was lost between them, nor between coaches Bubas and McGuire.

Heyman was fouled hard by Larry Brown, in front of the Carolina bench, at the opposite end of the floor where I was nestled in my now usual spot on the Duke bench. A fight erupted. It looked to me like Heyman was in trouble, down there in enemy territory. Duke fans were streaming onto the court.

Bubas pulled the Duke players back, and told us not to leave the bench. I disobeyed, concerned about Heyman's status.

Like Gulliver, in the land of the Brobdingnag, I slipped away and headed to where the action was. Yogi Poteet, the Carolina guard, had his fists up and was circling, expecting attackers from all sides. Doug Moe was under siege as well, from some of the more rabid Duke fans.

Heyman was all right, order was restored, and I drifted back to the bench.

Eddie Cameron and the Duke athletic officials claimed that the near-riot was North Carolina's fault. They stated that no Duke player even left the bench to join in the fray.

A careful review of game film, by ACC officials, revealed a little guy in jersey #24, wandering about amid the chaos.

Cameron wasn't happy. He asked me what in the hell I thought I was doing, heading down court to join the battle. I explained my concern about Heyman's well-being, but it didn't sell. He warned me never to do that again. I never did.

What can one say, when scolded by a legend?

CHAPTER SIX
THE 1960 CHAMPIONSHIP SEASON

The 1959-60 Duke basketball season opened at home, against Georgia Tech. Tech emphasized a relentless half-court pressure defense, which seemed to bother us and they prevailed, 59 to 49. I saw my first varsity action (figure 29), coming off the bench to score a basket and guarding a player named Roger Kaiser. After the game I thought to myself that if every player I had never heard of before was as tough as Kaiser, I would be in deep trouble. As it turned out, most were not of Roger's caliber; he went on to earn first-team all-American honors that year, and became the first Georgia Tech player to have his jersey retired.

Figure 29 - In action against Georgia Tech (my first game).

Two other Georgia Tech players intersected with me years later. Center Josh Powell sang in his beautiful baritone voice at my son's wedding. Guard Bobby Dews is one of the Atlanta Braves coaches now, and still teases me when I am the team doctor on call, reminding me of the whipping that his team gave us years before.

An early highlight was winning the pre-Christmas Birmingham Classic, thumping Alabama 78-60 and edging a scrappy Navy team by five points. Kistler, Youngkin, Hurt, Frye and Mullen played almost the entire games. I saw little action.

Right after Christmas, we faced top-ranked Utah in the first round of the Dixie Classic. They had an outstanding center, Billy "The Hill" McGill, and loved to play an up-tempo game. Assistant coach Shabel had scouted them, and deduced that they might be frustrated by a controlled, slowed-down pace. He was right, as we held McGill in check and won by 11. The joy was short-lived, however, as North Carolina pounded us 75 to 53 the next night, fueled by Lee Schaffer, Doug Moe, and York Larese. We subsequently lost again to Dayton the following evening, by eight.

I flew home for Christmas Eve, but had to return Christmas night for a practice session, to a largely deserted Duke campus.

We started the new year by smashing Bucknell 75 to 36, and then beat N.C. State and Clemson. The latter game was one of my best, as I came off the bench, in Clemson's bandbox-like gym, and made four of five jump shots despite a blaring brass student band that was seated right at courtside.

We played at North Carolina (figure 30) in early February. Coach Bubas thought a stall might work, but we quickly fell behind 10-0 and that ended the stalling. North Carolina beat us soundly again, 84 to 58.

Figure 30 - Versus U.N.C. during the regular season.

After that loss, Coach Bubas shook up the starting lineup, inserting me at guard and Fred Kast at forward and moving Howard Hurt up to the other guard spot. It was an awesome feeling, running out into darkened gyms under a spotlight as the announcer blared, "and starting at guard, from Shawano, Wisconsin, John Cantwell." Of the five games I started, we won two, both against Virginia, and lost to Maryland by 10, Wake Forest by 19, and in the regular season finale to North Carolina again by 25.

Coach Bubas went back to his "Birmingham Classic Five" for the tournament. It turned out to be a good move for the team, but as stated earlier, essentially ended any significant playing time for my subsequent college career.

We opened the ACC tournament with a 13 point win over South Carolina. Kistler led with 26 points and 10 rebounds, and Hurt added 21 points. I got in for a few minutes and contributed a free throw. The next night we stunned North Carolina, 71 to 69, avenging the three previous losses to them by 22, 26 and 25 point margins. Carroll Youngkin had an outstanding game with 30 points and 17 rebounds. Lee Schaffer got his fourth foul in the opening minutes of the second half, and could not mix it up with Youngkin as a result. Hurt and Frye hit clutch free throws down the stretch to preserve the victory. I was the only reserve to get in, spelling Mullen at the middle of our 1-1-3 zone defense for several minutes, and added a free throw.

In the championship game against Wake Forest, Frye again hit crucial free throws in the last minutes to give us a four point victory. Kistler led with 22 points (figure 31) and nine rebounds, outscoring Len Chappell. The post-game photo (figure 32) shows Mewhort, arms up raised, charging out to greet the regulars, and portly trainer, Gordon Johnson, setting a personal record with his vertical leap. Clutching our trophies in the post-game photo (figure 33) we were a happy lot.

Figure 31 – Kistler dunking against
Wake Forest. Billy Packer is on the left.

Figure 32 – Buzz Mewhort, manager Gordon Johnson, and others, celebrating our ACC championship.

Figure 33 – The 1960 ACC champions.

We moved on to Madison Square Garden, easily defeating Princeton by 24 points. Now down to the Sweet 16, we subdued St. Joseph's in Charlotte in a two point squeaker, led by Youngkin's 22 points and Hurt's 15. Mewhort was the only reserve to play, adding four points. St. Joseph's coach, Jack Ramsay, bitterly protested that the referee was slow in retrieving a ball Hurt had knocked out of bounds in the closing seconds.

We squared off against N.Y.U. the next night, to see who would go on the Final Four. N.Y.U. had a 21-3 record and was led by Tom "Satch" Sanders, a future Boston Celtics great. They had earned the right to face us with a one-point victory over West Virginia, despite Jerry West's 34 points.

The bubble burst against N.Y.U.. We simply ran out of gas. It was our sixth game in 10 days. We'd also had a 13-hour bus ride back from the Princeton game, because of a snowstorm. Plus, only five of our guys were playing almost the whole games. Sanders got his 22 points, as expected, almost matched by Kistler's 20, but it was an overweight forward as I recall who kept hitting key shots from the corner, keeping us from closing the gap.

As disappointing as the loss was to me, it probably preserved my pre-medical grade point average. It is almost impossible to keep up with laboratory courses such as organic chemistry and physics and miss days of school for tournament action. One of the chemistry projects was to synthesize a dove-white compound. The final day in the lab each student labeled the vial with his substance. There were various shades of white, and one dark blob, that looked like a melanotic stool. I turned in the product as far as I had been able to go. Needless to say, I got teased a lot about that. The professor understood my situation and gave me a D for the laboratory portion, dropping my overall grade in the course to a C.

During the summer of 1960 I went to summer school at the University of Wisconsin. I needed to take a pre-med course, embryology. I had a job at the Kappa Sigma fraternity house, waiting on tables, to pay for my room and board there. I roomed with my high school teammate, Marty Gharrity, who had just set a sophomore single season scoring record at Wisconsin, but was struggling with his grades.

I took him to the library with me once, supposedly to study. He didn't last long, peeling out to hit the Brathaus or the Varsity Bar.

He asked me to look over his term paper. "It looked okay," I said, "only you spelled indians in lower case about a hundred times." He changed it but it didn't help his grade point average and he later wound up at Northern Michigan University.

Politics were in the news during that summer, as Kennedy and Nixon were battling for the presidency. I had briefly seen Kennedy at Duke, on his campaign trail. He was handsome, youthful, vigorous and athletic, a contrast to the awkward, dour Nixon, with his perpetual five o'clock shadow. Like the rest of America, I would be stunned, just three years later (while in the wards of Cook County Hospital in Chicago) to hear of his assassination.

Every afternoon Gharrity and I, along with multiple others, gathered on one of Madison's outdoor basketball courts for several hours of scrimmaging. One of the fellows was D. Wayne Lucas, a classmate of my older brother's, who was taking graduate school courses and aspired to become a college basketball coach. He later gave that idea up to pursue his other love, horse training, where he has achieved triple crown success (although not all in the same year).

Everybody returned for the 1961 season, plus we added superstar Art Heyman, a 6'5" scoring and rebounding machine at guard. My playing time continued to plummet. I never particularly liked just getting into the game for the last spastic minute of an already decided contest, but soon discovered that there was something worse, not getting in at all, to even merit a post-game shower. A high ankle sprain in mid season practice added to my misery, and further limited my mobility. I decided to pass on my senior year and head off to medical school, beginning the nine-year process of becoming a cardiologist.

In reflecting upon the 1960 season, I am not surprised that we were able to turn things around in the tournament. In high school, as noted earlier, we lost two games to the worst team in our own conference, and yet rebounded to win 60 of the next 64 games.

CHAPTER SEVEN
EPILOGUE

In 1990 we gathered in Durham for a 30-year reunion (figure 34), a chance to reflect and to catch up on each other's lives. Howard Hurt (figure 35) received a Master's degree in education at Duke and did graduate work at the University of Virginia and at West Virginia University. He had two years of active duty in the Army and spent 18 years in the Army Reserve, retiring as a Major.

Figure 34 - The 30-year team reunion, 1990.

Figure 35 - Howard Hurt.

He has worked mainly in education, as a teacher, coach, principal and superintendent in North Carolina, Virginia and West Virginia. He is presently the CEO of Flying Eagle Enterprises, a team-building, relationship-building and motivational enhancing organization.

Married to Phyllis, from Farmville, North Carolina, Howard is the father of three sons and two daughters. His eldest, Fredrick, played college basketball at Lenoir Rhyne and currently coaches his younger brother, Howard, Jr., at the same high school that Carroll Youngkin attended in Winston-Salem, North Carolina.

Howard's son, Carlton, played football and basketball at Gardner Webb College, and his daughter, Adrianne, competed in basketball at Meredith.

The only 1960 team player still involved in competitive basketball, Howard and former Wake Forest players "Twig" Wiggins and Alley Hart, won the senior men's national basketball championship (3 on 3) in 2003.

Doug Albright (figure 36) got his law degree from American University. After two years of law practice he became the Assistant

District Attorney, the Chief District Prosecutor, the resident Superior Court Judge and (since 1984) the senior resident Superior Court Justice in North Carolina's 18th judicial district.

Figure 36 – Doug Albright.

He and his wife Mary (also from Greensboro) have four sons, each an accomplished athlete. Jon earned four varsity basketball letters at Memphis State, and has subsequently been a color commentator for Memphis State basketball telecasts, along with ESPN, CBS and other networks.

Eric was a three-year starter as a Duke second baseman.

Stuart was an all-state football lineman at Greensboro Senior High School and won four varsity letters at Duke as a football center and long snapper.

The youngest, Ethan, attended North Carolina where he lettered one year in baseball and four years in football as an offensive lineman. He made the all-ACC team and has spent 11 years in the National Football League, currently with the Washington Redskins.

Father Doug's exercise today involves walking and jogging, and various outdoor activities.

Larry Bateman (figure 37) worked in a purchasing career, initially with Collins and Aikman and then with Synthetic Industries, retiring in 1997.

Figure 37 – Larry Bateman.

Both of his sons attended the "rival" school, North Carolina. Larry's main sport now is tennis. He recently moved to Florida, arriving just in time for four hurricanes.

Fred Kast (figure 38) was in a medical supply capacity for the United States Air Force Reserve from 1963 to 1969. He worked in the healthcare industry for 37 years, in a sales and management capacity, for a company that was originally a division of American Hospital Supply, Inc. The company was involved in the manufacture, distribution and sales of intravenous solutions and associated products.

Fred retired in April, 1999. He still works as the official scorer for the Golden State Warriors, and has done so since 1963. His physical activities include tennis, bowling and occasional basketball "shoot-arounds."

Fred and his wife Anita have a son, Brian, and a daughter, Karen.

Figure 38 - Fred Kast.

C.B. Johnson (figure 39) attended Tulane Law School and did graduate law work at N.Y.U. He continues to practice law in New Orleans.

Figure 39 - C.B. Johnson.

His first wife, Pixie, died of breast cancer. He remarried, to Holly, in 2003 and is now a step-father to twin girls, age 13. C.B. has a daughter of his own, Cynthia, and two sons, Carter and Cameron. The latter was the only freshman to letter in high school varsity football, and was a running back on the team with his boyhood friend, Peyton Manning.

C.B.'s primary sport now is golf, in which he has a handicap of only 7.

Buzz Mewhort (figure 40) received his law degree from Duke in 1965. He is a partner with Shumaker, Loop and Kendrick, L.L.P., in Toledo, a 180 lawyer law firm with offices also in Columbus, Charlotte, and Tampa. Buzz has served as managing partner, chairman of the firm's management committee and head of their employment/labor law practice group.

Figure 40 – Buzz Mewhort.

He and his wife Martha (also a Duke graduate) have a son and two daughters. His son, Donald III, played at Wittenberg University for four years, including 119 straight games, as a 6'6" post man. Like his father, Don served as co-captain his senior year. His teams went to the NCAA division III Final Four in two of his four seasons and won 20 or more games each year. His coach, Larry Hunter, is now the assistant head coach at North Carolina State.

Buzz and Martha have enjoyed a variety of bicycling and hiking trips abroad, and also keep active with golf and tennis.

Merrill Morgan (figure 41) got his Master's degree in counseling at the University of Pennsylvania, and also has attended 30 other graduate courses from several colleges.

Figure 41 - Merrill Morgan.

He was an assistant treasurer at a savings and loan company, and then a history teacher and basketball coach at Woodbury, New Jersey, from 1963-67. In 1967, he moved to Col. Richardson High School in Federalsburg, Maryland, where he has been a guidance counselor and basketball coach. He retired from counseling in July, 2004, and from coaching in April, 2005.

He keeps active by playing basketball (like Howard Hurt and Jay Beal) and also enjoys running.

The Morgans have two sons and a daughter. All were multi-sport high school athletes. The sons graduated from the University of Maryland, while their daughter attended Duke.

Carroll Youngkin (figure 42) became the Chief Financial Officer for several companies, and currently sells real estate in Boca Raton, Florida.

Figure 42 – Carroll Youngkin.

He and his wife Ellis (who has a Ph.D. degree) have a son, Glenn, who had a basketball scholarship to Rice University, and a daughter, Dottie, who has a Master's degree in guidance counseling.

Jack Mullen (figure 43) was born with a defective aortic heart valve (two cusps instead of the usual three). Given his incredible physical stamina, it is hard to believe that anything could have been defective in his heart.

Figure 43 - Jack Mullen at age 49.

After graduating from Duke, Jack became the athletic director at a private boys school in Potomac, Maryland. He taught and coached for 10 years, and then went into carpentry, building furniture and remodeling homes. He also doubled as the tennis pro at a local country club and competed in tournaments.

He continued to play in a men's basketball league well into his 40s, and also enjoyed playing with his two sons, Steve and Jack. Steve (his father's look alike) played basketball and baseball in high school and continued with baseball at George Mason University. Jack Jr. played basketball and tennis in high school.

Jack Sr. underwent three open-heart surgery procedures in a two-year period. His last surgery was in 1983. He was feeling well and, in the week before his sudden death at age 52 from a ruptured thoracic aortic aneurysm, had even bought new basketball shoes to participate in the 1988 Duke alumni basketball game. The last picture his wife Karen took of Jack showed him standing on the basketball court, with his black lab dog, "Ebony."

Jack's nephew, Mike Brey, was an assistant basketball coach at Duke for seven years, and is now head coach at Notre Dame. The two oldest of Jack and Karen's three grandsons attended the Notre Dame basketball camp in the summer of 2005.

I now do cardiac examinations on all incoming freshman athletes at Georgia Tech. We do echocardiograms (ultrasound studies) on their hearts. One thing we look for is the valvular defect that caused Jack's early demise.

Doug Kistler (figure 44) was drafted by the Detroit Pistons in the NBA and by Hawaii in the ABA. Detroit placed him on waivers after the pre-season games, whereupon he was signed by the New York Knicks and played one season with them.

Figure 44 – Doug Kistler

He then worked as a sales rep with V. Mueller & Co. (American Hospital Supply), covering the eastern North Carolina region.

He subsequently became the first basketball coach at Jordan High School in Durham, N.C., and took the team to a perfect 28-0 season and the state championship, earning him Coach of the Year honors in North Carolina. He followed with coaching stints at Ravenscroft School in Raleigh and at Garringer High School in Charlotte.

Doug had two sons, Doug, Jr., ("Dee," who attended Appalachian State University), and Greg (a graduate of the University of North Carolina - Wilmington). Dee is 6'5" and played JV basketball, but had to stop because of joint problems. Like his dad, he is a drummer, and played in a college jazz band. Greg, a six-footer, ran track and played baseball. Both boys were also competitive swimmers.

Doug was killed by a drunken driver in February 1980, at the age of 41. Earlene eventually married Nelson Jackson and now lives in Myrtle Beach, S.C.

John Frye (figure 45) stayed at Duke for a while after graduation, received an M.A.T. degree, and taught and coached. He then obtained a Ph.D. in psychology at the University of Maryland and started a private practice, teaching and consulting in the business sector. He also does motivational speaking, like Howard Hurt.

Figure 45 – John Frye, Ph.D.

John and his ex-wife Phyllis had another son, Marc, and a daughter, Mechelle. After their divorce, Phyllis eventually remarried and lives near Marc and Mechelle in South Carolina.

John's two sons were good athletes in junior high school, but chose not to compete in high school, mainly due to lack of size and injuries. Mechelle became a track star, winning the state competition in the hurdles and the high jump and breaking the state record in the latter. She attended West Virginia University on a partial track scholarship and is now a chiropractor in Charlotte.

Young John got his Master's degree in computers, while Marc went into the building trade and has constructed over 1,200 homes to date.

Dr. John, and his partner, Ann Page Chiapella, Ph.D., (a Stanford graduate) are presently completing the Huntington Lodge, in Berkeley Springs, West Virginia. It will be available as a bed and breakfast and also as a facility for retreats and seminars. John's main sport today is golf, "with wine tasting a close second."

Jay Beal has been the hardest former teammate to track down. He didn't attend our 30-year reunion. Multiple mailings to the last address the Duke athletic office had on him went unanswered. Knowing that he was an attorney I tried to find him in my listing of lawyers, to no avail. I called his hometown in Connecticut, to see if a Jay Edwin Beal was listed in the telephone directory, also without success. No former teammate knew where he was, or had heard from him in years.

A friend told me about USsearch.com, which for a fee of $40.00 would attempt to find somebody for you. I anted up and received a phone number.

I spoke with Jay's second wife, Sherry. He was either at his real estate development office or at the gym, shooting hoops.

Jay didn't have children of his own, Sherry mentioned, but has been a good father to her three, also from a previous marriage. One is an emergency room physician.

Did Jay resent the teasing he received, which we were all subjected to? Was he mad that despite his deadly jump shot he didn't get to play much? Those questions remain unanswered.

I do know that he was a very happy guy, as we all were, one night in March, 1960, when our team performed up to our maximum potential to win the ACC tournament.

I left Duke after three years to start my medical school training at Northwestern, where I met a coed, Marilyn Moore, who became my wife during my senior year.

I continued to play basketball there on our medical fraternity team, and subsequently during an internship at the University of Florida (in a city league that featured Steve Spurrier) and during residency years at the Mayo Clinic.

Our son, Ryan, followed me to Duke, aided by a strong letter of recommendation from Vic Bubas. He competed in crew and served as senior class president. A physician now in the Atlanta area, he works with me as one of the team physicians for the Atlanta Braves.

My daughter, Kelly, competed in cross country at Denison, and subsequently went to nursing school. She lives in Atlanta also, with her husband and three young daughters.

My first-born son, Bradley, was severely retarded and never learned to speak. He did compete in the Special Olympics, bringing tears, joy and pride to his parents. He was a sweet little boy, deeply loved by his parents and siblings, and died of esophageal cancer at age 29.

I have kept active in the medical aspects of sports, as the team cardiologist for Georgia Tech (figure 46). In 1996, I also served as Chief Medical Officer for the Olympic Games, ultimately responsible for the care of 10,000 athletes and over 1.5 million spectators.

Figure 46 - John Cantwell, M.D.

I ran about five miles most days for nearly 30 years, until I had a hip replacement in July, 2001. I now walk an hour or so most days and enjoy hiking and biking trips with my wife, in various parts of the world.

Manager Gordon Johnson (figure 47) got a law degree from Tulane, and has been with the same law firm in New Orleans since 1963. He was the managing partner for 33 years, and assumed senior status in January 2005. He represents insurance and corporate defendants, in casualty litigation.

Figure 47 – Gordon Johnson.

He and his wife Marda have a son and two daughters, who graduated from Wake Forest, Rollins, and North Carolina respectively. Gordon's main activities today include fishing and golfing.

In his 10 seasons as head coach at Duke, Vic Bubas guided the teams to six straight 20-win seasons, three other ACC championships, and three Final Four appearances (1963, 1964, 1966). His teams won 76.1 percent of their games. Only legendary coach John Wooden had a better record in that decade. Eight of Vic's teams finished among the nation's top 10 in the final season ratings.

Nine of Vic's players went on to pro basketball careers. Twenty-nine of the 33 players he recruited received their degrees. Five of his assistants became head coaches, including Hubie Brown and Chuck Daly.

He became assistant to president Terry Sanford at Duke, and was instrumental in developing the Bryan Student Center there. After several years he became commissioner of the new Sunbelt Conference, bringing his organizational skills, integrity and commitment to aid in the development of those teams.

Retired now, the 77 year old Bubas (figure 48) lives with his wife and former high school sweetheart, Tootie, in Bluffton, South Carolina, where he enjoys spending time with his three red-headed daughters, 9 grandchildren and one great-grandchild (many of whom are or were athletes).

Figure 48 – Vic and Tootie Bubas with the bust of Eddie Cameron in between.

Duke honored him several years ago by naming one of their concourses in Cameron Indoor Stadium after him. He has also been enshrined in the North Carolina Sports Hall of Fame.

Assistant coach Fred Shabel (figure 49) has had a very successful business career after a head coaching stint for several years at Connecticut and an athletic directorship at the University of Pennsylvania. He has been chairman of the Comcast Spectacor Company, a Philadelphia-based sports and entertainment firm, which owns the Philadelphia 76ers of the NBA and the Philadelphia Flyers on the National Hockey League, among many other holdings. He has no plans to retire.

Figure 49 - Fred and Irene Shabel.

Fred and his wife Irene have a daughter, Lisa and a son, Alan.

After head coaching stints at West Virginia, (69-41 record), and at Duke (63-45 record), Bucky Waters (figure 50) became Vice Chancellor of the Duke Medical Center, heavily involved in fund raising. He co-founded the Duke Children's Classic, which to date has earned over 12 million dollars for the medical center. For this and other achievements, Bucky received an honorary Doctor of Medicine degree from Duke. He adds that he is only allowed to make one house call - to his own home. Retired from Duke now, he still works with ESPN TV and Westwood One CBS Radio as an announcer for college basketball games, and has covered professional golf, baseball, and tennis, along with the 1988 Olympics. North

Carolina State gave him their Distinguished Alumnus Award in 2001. In March, 2005, he received the Lou Gehrig/Catfish Hunter Humanitarian Award.

Figure 50 – Bucky and Dottie Waters.

As head coach at West Virginia, he guided his team to an upset victory over Vic Bubas's undefeated Duke squad in 1966, when the latter was ranked #1 in the nation.

Bucky's son and two daughters were active in high school basketball, volleyball and tennis respectively.

His sporting endeavors today include golf and tennis.

He and his wife Dottie (who reminded me of movie starlet Debbie Reynolds in my college days) have been married about 50 years.

Among his many memories of the 1960 ACC championship run was during a time out in the final game. While trying to diagram an inbounds play to seal the victory, Bucky had water spilled over his shoulder by manager Gordon Johnson: "It was funny...later."

What did I learn from my college basketball experience?

I learned that I could complete at the highest level, even though the results weren't as productive as I'd hoped. One of the few personal highlights my junior year was to guard Art Heyman (figure 51) in practice sessions. As Pat Conroy described Art (in "My Losing Season") his game "was urban black, big city, kiss my ass and hold the mayo, in your face wise-ass Jewish, no holds barred and a hot dog at Nathan's after the game." In his senior year, Heyman was voted the nation's top player.

Figure 51 - Art Heyman.

I also observed again, as in high school, that one season has many facets. You have to pick yourself up after a loss, retain your self-confidence, and figure out a way to win the next time. It is also important to peak at the right time, namely as tournament time approaches.

Exposure to coach Vic Bubas was an education in itself, observing how he handled others (including the tempestuous Heyman), was superbly organized, utilized every second of your time, and was there for you after you graduated in case you ever needed a good word. I am sure his letter to the Mayo Clinic was of help in getting me a medicine residency at that prestigious institution.

I learned that dreams need to be tempered sometimes by reality. With superstar freshman, Jeff Mullins (figure 52), a future Olympic gold medalist and all-pro performer joining our team, my playing time would have been negligible had I stayed on for my senior year. It was time to move on, to start the long road to becoming a cardiologist.

*Figure 52 – Jeff Mullins (all-American, all-pro,
Olympic gold medalist) in recent years.*

I had a great experience, getting to play in the NCAA tournament, the Dixie Classic, and several times in Madison Square Garden. I got to see the best side of college basketball, the excellent players and quality coaches like Vic Bubas. I also saw basketball at its worst, playing in games against Seton Hall and North Carolina State that were fixed.

Could I have played today? The game has certainly changed, with the addition of black athletes (who weren't allowed to attend Duke or to play in the ACC in 1960), cross-over dribbles, tattoos, long, baggy pants, and guards who can swoop in toward the basket and slam down a dunk with their non-dominant hand, and full-court zone presses the entire game. The shooting eyes of current players aren't any better (except for a few, like Duke's J.J. Redick), but the players certainly are. I have seen some team members in the

ACC the past few years who reminded me of myself, but they rarely played much, except in blowout situations.

I do have the satisfaction of knowing that my Duke jersey (#24) has been retired by the school. Johnny Dawkins and I combined for over 2,650 points while wearing that number. If truth be told, all but 114 points were made by Johnny, Duke's career scoring leader.

I have done a medical examination on Coach Bubas in recent years. The Devil (? Blue) suggested that I be a little rough with certain parts of the procedure, whispering in my ear how hard practices had been and how little I got to play in my junior year. I brushed any such thoughts aside and went easy on Vic, remembering all the positive things he taught me, both in words and in deeds.

I still shoot around sometimes, despite the hip replacement several years ago. In games of horse with my son, he will ask me what kind of a shot I made. "A jump shot from here," I'd answer. "No, it wasn't a jump shot," he'd respond, "your feet never left the ground."

Once in a while, shooting alone, my mind will drift back to the 1960 season at Duke. I will recall all the great players we had to face, such as Billy Packer and Len Chappell at Wake Forest and York Larese, Doug Moe and Lee Schaffer of North Carolina, and I will break into a grin, recalling that magical three nights one March when we played like we had never played before.

AFTERWORD
By Coach Vic Bubas

In his recent book on One Hundred Seasons of Duke Basketball, Bill Brill notes that Coach Bubas called "the 1960 team his favorite because it overcame so many obstacles to win the school's first ACC championship." He also considered the win over UNC in that year's ACC tournament to be one of his greatest victories.

I asked Coach Bubas to write an afterword for this book. He preferred to focus on the team, rather than on individuals, fearful that he might slight someone. His focus was appropriate, for we played as a team, and won as a team:

"When I was appointed the Head Basketball Coach at Duke University, it was not to resurrect Duke's basketball program. Duke was good before I got there in the spring of 1959. In various years prior to that, Duke had won regular season titles and had a good record against N.C. State, where I had played my college basketball and had been an assistant coach for eight years. I perceived my job to be getting the Blue Devils to the NCAA Tourney, which meant winning the ACC tournament. Duke's previous head coach, Hal Bradley, had left Duke to accept the position of head basketball coach at the University of Texas. He was not fired by Duke; he felt Texas gave him a better opportunity to succeed.

In 1959, in order to play in the NCAA tournament, a team had to win the ACC tournament. The ACC tournament winner was declared the champion. There was no immediate help because freshman were not eligible to play on the varsity team. They had to play freshman ball. The team we inherited was good, had talented athletes and good students, smart basketball players, and anxious to learn. Any new and young coach (I was 32 years old at the time) always wonders how he'll be accepted, but this team made it easy for me. As we moved along, it was a learning process for all of us. We knew some of our tactics were different and hopefully better, but it was 'our way' and it was our job to sell it to the team.

One of the luckiest outcomes of the change of coaches at Duke in 1959 was that I had to accept the assistant coaches. I could not bring in my own assistants. The assistants were Fred Shabel and Whit Cobb. During my initial summer at Duke, Whit Cobb informed me that he wanted to go into the investment business and would leave coaching. During that summer, I hired Raymond 'Bucky' Waters who played under Everett Case and me at N.C. State and was then a high school coach in western North Carolina. Fred Shabel was a great communicator and he knew Duke University. He graduated from Duke and knew how demanding it was academically to be a student at Duke. He was involved in the recruiting of the players who would play for us. Bucky knew what it was like to be in a basketball program under Everett Case. It was an aggressive and highly organized program, and that is where we wanted to take our team at Duke. Both Fred and Bucky were good coaches, good communicators and I was lucky to have them. We could not have achieved what we did without their contributions. They went on to distinguished themselves as head coaches after they left Duke... Bucky at West Virginia and Fred at the University of Connecticut.

During the course of the first season, we were thrashed and humiliated by North Carolina three times and by Wake Forest twice. All five of those defeats were by about 20 points each. The team, however, was getting better in a number of little things on offense and defense. I thought we had a good chance of winning the ACC tournament in Raleigh if we could limit our turnovers and hit a good percentage of field goals and free throws. In a moment of exuberance at a media event, I predicted we would win it. Our confidence was high and after winning the first game in the 1960 tournament, we were paired against North Carolina in the semifinals. We used a 1-1-3 zone defense that Wake Forest Coach Bones McKinney taught me and had used against us and a few other teams. We had a fast, strong guard (Jack Mullen) playing in the middle of that defense and his great speed and quickness allowed him to cover both corners and the middle. We beat North Carolina in that game and surprised many who believed that we had no chance. I felt we had beaten a team good enough to make it to the Final Four in the NCAA Tourney, and maybe win it all. We then played against Wake Forest in the championship game, used the same defense, and won again. We were heading towards the NCAA tournament after a mediocre season, but now with the conference championship trophy in our hands.

Our team headed for New York to meet Princeton in Madison Square Garden in the first round of the NCAA. We beat Princeton and went on to Charlotte and the Sweet Sixteen. In Charlotte we beat a very good St. Joseph's team coached by Jack Ramsey. We were in the Elite Eight, playing for a spot in the Final Four. We were matched against N.Y.U. who had Satch Sanders; they beat Duke and our Cinderella story was over. This team proved what it was to dream, hope, work hard, and believe.

The '59-'60 team was a collection of young men who had the character and intelligence to be a huge success later in life. They went on to become lawyers, doctors, businessmen, teachers, preachers, judges and coaches. Again, how lucky was I who had these young men handed to me in my first year??

One of the great joys I have in life is to see those men and their families after they leave Duke. I am so proud of them, and I am grateful for their leadership in taking Duke to the next level. Little did I know that they would initiate a process that would take other teams in the 60s to new heights that would include three Final Fours and many top ten ratings. They hold a special place in my heart."

The 50-Year Reunion

The Duke University Athletic Department honored us on January 3, 2010, the 50th anniversary of the school's first ACC championship.

Coach Vic Bubas and his wife Tootie hosted us at a luncheon at the posh Washington Duke Hotel. Vic thanked us for jump-starting his coaching career and gave each of us a signed picture, indicating that we "set the pace" for future Duke basketball success.

Ten players attended, along with assistant coach Bucky Waters and manager Gordon Johnson. Sadly, Jay Beal again failed to appear, his loss as well as ours. We posed for a few pictures (fig. 53, 54).

That evening we attended a cocktail reception at the Schwartz-Butters Athletic Building, just prior to the Duke-Clemson game. A picture of our team was on the cover of the game program. We were all introduced at halftime (fig. 55) and even signed autographs after the game. The biggest fan applause went appropriately to Coach Bubas, who took his teams to three Final Fours in 10 years and our team to the Final Eight.

Because of hip surgery I missed the biggest men's basketball reunion in the school's history, held on February 12-13, 2010, in honor of Coach Mike Krzyzewski's 1000th game in 30 years (and the 70 years of legendary basketball in Cameron Indoor Stadium). Over 300 former players, managers, coaches and trainers attended.

Figure 53 - Our team 50-years later.

Figure 54 - With Coach Bubas, son Ryan, grandchildren Cameron and Hannah, at the pre-game reception.

Figure 55 - Being recognized at halftime of the Duke-Clemson Game

APPENDIX 1

DUKE'S FIRST ACC
CHAMPIONS: 1960

*Figure 56 – The 1960 Duke Team. (Left to right:
Cantwell, Mullen, Morgan, Johnson, Mewhort, Bateman,
Kast, Kistler, Youngkin, Albright, Hurt, Beal, Frye.)*

John Davis Cantwell, M.D.

THE 1960 DUKE BASKETBALL ROSTER (Figure 53)

Head Coach: VIC BUBAS

No.	Name	Age	Ht.	Wt.	Class	Hometown
15	Fred Kast - C-F	20	6-7	200	Jr.	Rahway, N.J.
20	Jack Mullen - G	24	5-11	170	So.	Weissport, Pa.
21	Howard Hurt - F	20	6-2	175	Jr.	Beckley, W. Va.
23	Carroll Youngkin - C	21	6-6	210	Jr.	Winston-Salem, N.C.
24	John Cantwell - G	19	5-9	180	So.	Shawano, Wisc.
25	C.B. Johnson - F	19	6-3	185	So.	New Orleans, La.
30	John Frye - G	20	5-11	170	Jr.	Huntington, W. Va.
31	Doug Albright - F	20	6-4	200	Jr.	Greensboro, N.C.
32	Merrill Morgan - G	21	6-3	175	Jr.	Montclair, N.J.
33	Larry Bateman - C	26	6-6	215	Sr.	Durham, N.C.
35	Buzz Mewhort - F	19	6-4	200	So.	Toledo, Ohio
40	Jay Beal - G	21	5-10	160	Jr.	Wethersfield, Conn.
41	Doug Kistler - F	21	6-8	205	Jr.	Wayne, Pa.

Figure 57 - The 1960 ACC championship banner that hangs from the rafters in Cameron Indoor Stadium.

86

ABOUT THE AUTHOR

John D. Cantwell, M.D., practices cardiology in Atlanta, where he enjoys hanging out with his wife, two children, and six grandchildren.

A team physician for the Atlanta Braves since 1976, he also serves as team cardiologist for Georgia Tech. In 1996 he was Chief Medical Officer for the Olympic Games.

A member of the Explorers Club, Dr. Cantwell has enjoyed adventure travels on all seven continents.

He is a charter member of his high school's sports Hall of Fame, and still holds the career basketball scoring record, set in the two-point era nearly a half-century ago.

Duke retired his jersey number after he and Johnny Dawkins combined for 2,670 career points (all but 114 thanks to the left-hander).

Made in the USA
Coppell, TX
06 December 2020

42782576R00066